Schlof gutt, klenge Wollef

Sleep Tight, Little Wolf

E Billerbuch an zwou Sproochen

Ulrich Renz · Barbara Brinkmann

Schlof gutt, klenge Wollef

Sleep Tight, Little Wolf

Iwwersetzung:

Maurice P. Heinz (Lëtzebuergesch)

Pete Savill (Englesch)

Audio a Video:

www.sefa-bilingual.com/bonus

Password for free access:

Lëtzebuergesch: **Sorry, audio or video is not yet available in this language.**

Englesch: **LWEN1423**

We are currently working on making as many of our bilingual books as possible available to you as audio books and videos. We kindly ask for your patience if there is no audio or video version in your language yet! You can keep up with the progress of our work on our website:
www.sefa-bilingual.com/languages

Gutt Nuecht, Tim! Mir siche muer weider.

Schlof lo gutt!

Good night, Tim! We'll continue searching tomorrow.

Now sleep tight!

Dobaussen ass et schonn däischter.

It is already dark outside.

Wat mécht den Tim dann do?

What is Tim doing?

E geet eraus, op d'Spillplaz.

Wat sicht hien do?

He is leaving for the playground.

What is he looking for there?

De klenge Wollef!

Ouni dee kann hien net schlofen.

The little wolf!

He can't sleep without it.

Wie kënnt dann do?

Who's this coming?

D'Marie! Hatt sicht säi Ball.

Marie! She's looking for her ball.

A wat sicht den Tobi?

And what is Tobi looking for?

Säi Bagger.

His digger.

A wat sicht d'Nala?

And what is Nala looking for?

Seng Popp.

Her doll.

Mussen d'Kanner net an d'Bett?

D'Kaz wonnert sech nawell.

Don't the children have to go to bed?

The cat is rather surprised.

Wie kënnt dann elo?

Who's coming now?

Dem Tim seng Mama a säi Papa!

Ouni hiren Tim kënne si net schlofen.

Tim's mum and dad!

They can't sleep without their Tim.

An do kommen der nach méi! Dem Marie säi Papp.
Dem Tobi säi Bopa. An dem Nala seng Mamm.

More of them are coming! Marie's dad.
Tobi's grandpa. And Nala's mum.

Lo awer séier an d'Bett!

Now hurry to bed everyone!

Gutt Nuecht, Tim!

Muer musse mer net méi sichen.

Good night, Tim!

Tomorrow we won't have to search any longer.

„Schlof gutt, klenge Wollef!"

Sleep tight, little wolf!

D 'Auteuren

Ulrich Renz was born in Stuttgart, Germany, in 1960. After studying French literature in Paris he graduated from medical school in Lübeck and worked as head of a scientific publishing company. He is now a writer of non-fiction books as well as children's fiction books.

www.ulrichrenz.de

Barbara Brinkmann was born in Munich in 1969 and grew up in the foothills of the Bavarian Alps. She studied architecture in Munich and is currently a research associate in the Department of Architecture at the Technical University of Munich. She also works as a freelance graphic designer, illustrator, and author.

www.bcbrinkmann.de

Do you like drawing?

Here are the pictures from the story to color in:

www.sefa-bilingual.com/coloring

Enjoy!

Ulrich Renz · Marc Robitzky

The Wild Swans
Les cygnes sauvages

Based on a fairy tale by

Hans Christian Andersen

+ audio   + video

English   bilingual   **French**

D'wëll Schwanen

E Mäerchen nom Hans Christian Andersen

► Fir Kanner vu 4-5 Joer a méi

„D'Wëll Schwanen" vum Hans Christian Andersen ass net fir näischt eent vun deene Märecher, déi weltwäit am meeschte gelies ginn. Seng zäitlos Form thematiséiert de Stoff, aus dem all eis mënschlech Drame sinn: Angscht, Mutt, Léift, Verrod, Trennung a Sech-Erëmfannen.

Erhältlech an Är Sproochen?

► Frot eise „Sproochenassistent":

www.sefa-bilingual.com/languages

My Most Beautiful Dream

► Reading age: 2-3 and up

Lulu can't fall asleep. All her cuddly toys are dreaming already – the shark, the elephant, the little mouse, the dragon, the kangaroo, and the lion cub. Even the bear has trouble keeping his eyes open...

Hey bear, will you take me along into your dream?

Thus begins a journey for Lulu that leads her through the dreams of her cuddly toys – and finally to her own most beautiful dream.

Erhältlech an Är Sproochen?

► Frot eise „Sproochenassistent":

www.sefa-bilingual.com/languages

Special thanks for his IT support to our son, Paul Bödeker, Freiburg, Germany

ISBN: 9783739900568

www.ingramcontent.com/pod-product-compliance
Lightning Source LLC
Chambersburg PA
CBHW041444120626
46547CB00002B/337